Other books by Luis J. Rodríguez

Poetry:

Poems Across the Pavement (1989)
The Concrete River (1991)

Memoir:

Always Running: La Vida Loca, Gang Days in L.A. (1993)

Children's Book:

América Is Her Name (1998)

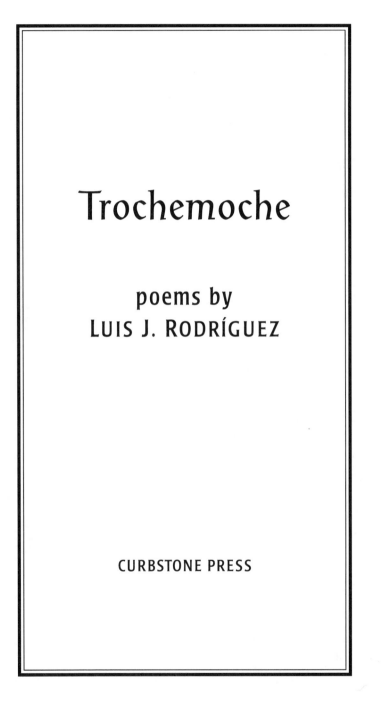

Trochemoche

poems by
Luis J. Rodríguez

CURBSTONE PRESS

Printed in Canada on acid-free paper by Best Book Manufacturers
Cover design: Stephanie Church

This book was published with the support of the Connecticut
Commission on the Arts, the National Endowment for the Arts, and
donations from many individuals. We are very grateful for this support.
The publishers also thank Lisa Farino and Ellen Partridge for their help
with layout and proofing.

Library of Congress Cataloging-in-Publication Data
    Rodríguez, Luis J., 1954-
        Trochemoche : poems / by Luis J. Rodríguez. — lst ed.
            p.   cm.
        ISBN 1-880684-50-0   (pbk : alk. paper)
        1. Mexican Americans—Poetry. I. Title.
        PS3568.034879T76   1998
        811'.54—dc21   98-9201

published by
CURBSTONE PRESS   321 Jackson Street   Willimantic, CT 06226
phone: (860) 423-5110   e-mail: curbston@connix.com
www.connix.com/~curbston/

Some of the poems in this collection were previously published in the following anthologies and publications (sometimes in different versions than collected here): *Shards of Light/Astillas de luz,* edited by Olivia Maciel; *El Coro,* edited by Martín Espada; *Aloud: Voices from the Nuyorican Cafe,* edited by Bob Holman and Miguel Algarin; *Currents from the Dancing River: Contemporary Latino Fiction, Nonfiction and Poetry,* edited by Ray González; *Shakespeare & Company: Biography of a Bookstore in Picture & Poems,* edited by Sylvia Beach Whitman (Paris); *Slam Poetry: Heftige Dichtung Aus Amerika* (German translation; Berlin); *Unsettling America: An Anthology of Contemporary Multicultural Poetry,* edited by Maria Mazziotti Gillan and Jennifer Gillan; *Identity Lessons: Learning American Style, An Anthology of Contemporary Writing,* edited by Maria Mazziotti Gillan and Jennifer Gillan; *Bloomsbury Review; The Carolina Quarterly; Catechumenate: A Journal of Christian Initiation; Colorado Review; Crosswinds Magazine; Ergo: The Bumpershoot Literary Magazine; Forkroads: A Journal of Ethnic American Literature; Green Mountain Review; Guadalupe Review; Hyphen Magazine; Jackleg; Long Shot; The Nation; Pemmican; People's Tribune; Poetry Flash; Poetry U.S.A.; San Fernando Poetry Journal; Strong Coffee; Tamaqua; TriQuarterly; Willow Review.*

Special thanks to the Lila Wallace-Reader's Digest Fund, the Lannan Foundation, the Mosaic Multicultural Foundation, the Illinois Arts Council, the Chicago Department of Cultural Affairs, the Guild Complex and Tía Chucha Press, Irene's Place, Chicago Teachers' Center, Youth Struggling for Survival, Rock-a-Mole!, the Chicago Coalition for the Homeless and, of course, Sandy Taylor and Judy Doyle of Curbstone Press for their support of my poetry.

This book is dedicated
to Trini

CONTENTS

I. My Beautiful Whisper

II. Poems Too Short to Braid

III. Notes of a Bald Cricket

trochemoche /trot-ch'e-mot-ch'e/ *adv*. (Span.; fam.)
1: helter-skelter, pell mell; all over the place. 2: haphazard;
inconsiderate.

Preface: "Poetry By the Laws of Nature"

"Live the life you have imagined."
—Henry David Thoreau

Poetry, like any art, touches all creation, all life. Not just the intense experiences but also the mundane. You can find poetry in the cracks along a wall, in the faces of friends, in the palms of children—in the *trochemoche* of our manifold existence. As well as a means of expression, poetry is a way of knowledge, of participation in the world, of discovering, as Henry James charged, "the significance in all things."

Not long ago, I facilitated weekly poetry workshops at an arts-based shelter for homeless women in Chicago, most of them with the help of performance poet Cin Salach. Although the women consisted of former employees, housewives and mothers, many intelligent and skilled, some of them were considered "hard-core" homeless—substance abusers, mentally ill; a few had been raped and terribly scarred, emotionally as well as bodily. Yet what was to be a six-week program ended up lasting four years. The women wouldn't let me go—and for so long I couldn't let them go.

I opened up to a deeper level of poetry, a word-dance that traveled the path of spirit yet remained tethered to the mother ground we all walk on. These women proved that a person's value is not dependent on whether one has a job, a spouse, children or even a home; that it's not based on material wealth (or the lack of it), skin color, or sexual orientation. What gives us "value" is that we are human, possessing intrinsic attributes waiting to be nurtured, developed and guided. There abides in every person a reservoir of creativity that when tapped proves to be inexhaustible. As the saying goes, "artists are not a special kind of person; every person is a special kind of artist."

1

Yet the artist in each of us is too often corralled, dissuaded, or suppressed.

So when everything else has been taken away from them, the women struggle to maintain their core being—which is mind linked to desire linked to necessity (one of the women called this "poetry by the laws of nature"). There is nothing more powerful and transformative in a human being than an awakened heart, an engaged imagination, the clarity of purpose associated with conscious life-activity.

This was evident in workshops I conducted throughout the country—from behind thick-walled cells in the juvenile halls of Santa Cruz or Tucson to maximum security prisons in California or Connecticut; from "classrooms" in El Paso held in cluttered storage rooms beneath aging bleachers to private schools along the mansion-strewn Main Line of Bryn Mawr, PA; from the most over-crowded schools in the country (in East L.A.) to some of the most sparse (next to corn fields in Nebraska); among Puerto Rican migrant workers in upstate New York to impoverished Southeast Asian youth in Fresno; from rez's such as the Quinault in Washington state to the Navajo in northeast Arizona; from among poor white youth in the depressed east Ohio coal-and-steel valleys to Mexican immigrant children in Chicago's Pilsen *barrio*.

So why is poetry today mostly missing from our lives? I believe this is due to the soul-death that is implicit in the modern, high-tech but economically and socially archaic capitalist order that exists in the United States of America.

With all my revolutionary heart and mind, I declare love for this land, its people and its destiny. Within these shores flow the blood of the Swanee, the Chumash, the Tohono O'Odham, the Irish dockworker, the Yoruba drummer, the Yiddish-speaking dressmaker, the African American journalist, the Hungarian packing-shed worker—from former slaves to former farmers, autoworkers to deep sea fishermen, soldiers to teachers, Bavarian shopkeepers to Dominican preachers, Gypsies to Salvadoran refugees, Wobblies to Muslims, Huicholes to the Hmong.

But I know, like all empires before, this country will be crushed by the weight of its own deceptions unless we turn toward the outcasts, the abandoned, like the women at the shelter, to witness essential humanity stirring and free even if, for the moment, imprisoned by circumstance and history.

I'd like to recognize a few of the great writers who recently passed on and who accomplished this in their own way: Meridel Le Sueur, Denise Levertov, José Antonio Burciaga, Ricardo Sanchez, Melvin Dixon, and Allen Ginsburg.

I believe in the cooperative, equitable, and abundant place this country is capable of becoming (and that once existed for most of my ancestors, the original peoples of this land). A vital step is to realize the abundance within our own souls.

Poetry may not get us there, but it can help illuminate the way.

— Luis J. Rodríguez
Chicago / December 1996

I

My Beautiful Whisper

Meeting the Animal in Washington Square Park

The acrobats were out in Washington Square Park,
flaying arms and colors: the jokers and break
dancers, the singers and mimes. I pulled out
of a reading at New York City College
and watched a crowd gather around a young man
jumping over 10 garbage cans from a skateboard.
Then out of the side of my eye I saw someone
who didn't seem to belong here, like I didn't
belong. He was a big man, six feet and more,
with tattoos on his arms, back, stomach and neck.
On his abdomen were the words in huge old English
lettering: Hazard. I knew this guy, I knew that place.
I looked closer. It had to be him. It was—Animal!
From East L.A. World heavyweight contender,
the only Chicano from L.A. ever ranked
in the top ten of the division. The one who
went toe-to-toe with Leon Spinks and even
made Muhammad Ali look the other way.
Animal! I yelled. "Who the fuck are you?" he asked,
a quart of beer in his grasp, eyes squinting.
My name's Louie—from East L.A. He brightened. "East L.A.!
Here in Washington Square Park? Man, we everywhere!"
The proverbial "what part of East L.A.?" came next.
But I gave him a shock. From La Gerahty, I said.
That's the mortal enemy of the Big Hazard
gang of the Ramona Gardens Housing Projects.
"I should kill you," Animal replied. If we were in
L.A., I suppose you would—but we in New York City, man.
"I should kill you anyway."
Instead he thrust out his hand with the beer and offered
me a drink. We talked—about what happened since he stopped
boxing. About the time I saw him at the Cleland House

arena looking over some up-and-coming fighters.
How he had been to prison, and later ended up homeless
in New York City, with a couple of kids somewhere.
And there he was, with a mortal enemy from East L.A.,
talking away. I told him how I was now a poet,
doing a reading at City College, and he didn't wince
or looked surprised. Seemed natural. Sure. A poet
from East L.A. That's the way it should be. Poet
and boxer. Drinking beer. Among the homeless,
the tourists and acrobats. Mortal enemies.
When I told him I had to leave, he said "go then,"
but soon shook my hand, East L.A. style, and walked off.
"Maybe, someday, you'll do a poem about me, eh?"
Sure, Animal, that sounds great.
Someday, I'll do a poem about you.

Victory, Victoria, My Beautiful Whisper

(for Andrea Victoria)

You are the daughter who is sleep's beauty.
You are the woman who birthed my face.
You are a cloud creeping across the shadows,
drenching sorrows into heart-sea's terrain.
Victory, Victoria, my beautiful whisper:
how as a baby you laughed into my neck
when I cried at your leaving
after your mother and I broke up;
how at age three you woke me up from stupid
so I would stop peeing into your toy box
in a stupor of resentment and beer;
and how later, at age five, when I moved in
with another woman who had a daughter about your age,
you asked: "how come *she* gets to live with Daddy?"
        Muñeca, these words cannot traverse the stone
path of our distance; they cannot take back the thorns
of falling roses that greet your awakenings.
These words are from places too wild for hearts to gallop,
too cruel for illusions, too dead for your eternal
gathering of flowers. But here they are, weary offerings
from your appointed father, your anointed man-guide;
make of them your heart's bed.

Street Talk

(Overheard among street people in Berkeley, October 1990)

The rag-faced woman sneered at the shriveled man:
"What do you know about pain,
about unwashed nights and the color-knife
tearing up your flesh.
You ain't black?
You ain't been through nothing."

The man replied in poison tones:
"I've been through 'nam, sister;
I've seen dudes sliced in half,
heads on bamboo poles.
You ain't been to 'nam,
man, you ain't seen shit."

The woman waved her arms, walked up
to the man in soil-striped pants:
"Get out my face, whitey, I'm a descendent
of slaves; I've seen lynchings; I've
seen castrated dicks dangle from bodies.
Don't talk to me about no 'nam!"

The man stepped toward her, ears
bursting with red indignation:
"Yeah, you think you've felt the knife-twist!
Walk in my shoes, lady; see what I've seen.
Bombs tearing up your feet.
Make you wish you could be black."

The woman shrieked: "Fuck you then!"

"Shit, what do you know?" replied the man.

Catacombs

The concave view over desert groves
 is maligned, dense with sacrifices
 not to be believed.
A native face peers backward to time
 and woman, gathering memory like
 flowers on healing cactus.
Your eye is froth & formation, it is
 rain of protocol you can't relinquish
 as water is wasted on sacred sand.

Across the turquoise rug, hexagon shapes.

I discover you, the howl of eternal mornings
 while beckoning the blue from this sky,
 while gesturing an infant from sleeping tree.
Sip the maguey juice from these mountains,
 shear chaos from the catacombs:
 forget and ferment the pain.

On the back of your hand, circles of flame.

A Tale of Los Lobos

One summer, to watch Los Lobos play,
I drove several hundred miles
from Chicago to Charleston,
West Virginia with three
Chicano buddies: Geronimo,
Mitch, and Dario.
We got there in time to catch
a great concert. Afterwards,
we went backstage and talked
to the band members.
We told the band we'd see them
later at the honky tonk club
where they were expected to perform.
But they had to leave right away
and couldn't make it.
We arrived at the club, sans Lobos,
and the place was packed.
I didn't think there'd be a seat,
but soon someone directed us to a table
where three pitchers of beer stood
at attention on the varnished table top.
Great service, I thought. We sat down,
poured beers into frosty glasses,
and took in the down-home blues
emanating from the small, smoke-filled stage.
Before we finished the pitchers,
three more were brought over
(although nobody had asked for our money!)
So we drank away, enjoying ourselves,
the only Mexicans in the place.
What gives? I asked. Geronimo, Mitch and Dario
shrugged their shoulders.

Soon many eyes turned our way.
Something's up, I whispered,
look at the way everybody's looking at us.
Sure enough, the band stopped and someone
at the mike asked us to come up to the stage.
"¡*Que cabula*!" Mitch exclaimed, "they think
we're Los Lobos!"
Damn, man, I said, we don't even look like them!
Geronimo stood up, said he was sorry
but we weren't Los Lobos, and sat down.
Everything stopped. Incredulous stares
surrounded us. After an embarrassing
silence, the house band began
a slow number, than upped the tempo,
finally rocking the place
with harmonica-laden fervor.
Hijo de su, they believe us, I said.
"I don't know," Dario replied,
"I think they think we're lying."
One dude approached us:
"I know you're Los Lobos;
you just don't want to play, right?"
No, for reals, we ain't them, I responded.
He winked and kept on walking.
When I went to the restroom,
a woman by the phone stopped me:
"I liked the way you played guitar
at the gig earlier."
That wasn't me, I explained.
"What I want to know," the girl then asked,
"is how you got rid of the goatee so fast."
I took my piss and rushed back to my seat.
Rumors that we were Los Lobos abounded.
Some shouted for us to get off it and perform.
"If we did," Geronimo quipped, "Los Lobos

would never play this town again."
I then noticed a bevy of West Virginia beauties,
local groupies, who followed the out-of-town
bands that landed here. They wouldn't leave
even after we gave them expressions that said:
you're nice, but we ain't them!
One girl who sat directly behind me
had on a prom dress! She kept
ordering gin-and-tonics, waiting for a signal
from one of us, I presumed, for her
to join us at the table. We decided not to go
this route. Mitch figured we may have to scram
if people here concluded we had
insulted their fair city, club, and women.
All our denials seemed pointless,
resulting in more knowing winks
as if they were all in on our little joke.
The pitchers kept coming,
the house band coaxed us up
once or twice,
and the groupies held on
like real troopers.
Finally, people began to depart.
The band packed up its instruments
and most of the girls had split.
Then just before our last beer,
a loud thump exploded behind me.
I turned. The girl in the party dress
had fallen over in her chair,
drunker than shit! We helped her back
on the stool. My partners and I
promptly left the club as quietly as we could
on the night Los Lobos didn't play
in Charleston, West Virginia.

Cinco de Mayo

Cinco de Mayo celebrates a burning people,
those whose land is starved of blood,
civilizations which are no longer
holders of the night. We reconquer with our feet,
with our tongues, that dangerous language,
saying more of this world than the volumes
of textured and controlled words on a page.
We are the gentle rage; our hands hold
the steam of the earth, the flowers
of dead cities, the green of butterfly wings.
Cinco de Mayo is about the barefoot, the untooled,
the warriors of want who took on the greatest army
Europe ever mustered—and won.
I once saw a Mexican man stretched across
an upturned sidewalk
near Chicago's 18th and Bishop one fifth of May day.
He brought up a near-empty bottle
to the withering sky and yelled out a *grito*
with the words: ¡*Que viva Cinco de Mayo*!
And I knew then what it meant—
what it meant for barefoot Zapoteca *indigenas*
in the Battle of Puebla and what it meant for me
there on 18th Street among *los ancianos*,
the moon-faced children and futureless youth
dodging gunfire and careening battered cars,
and it brought me to that war
that never ends, the war Cinco de Mayo
was a battle of, that I keep fighting,
that we keep bleeding for, that war
against our servitude that a *compa*
on 18th Street knew all about
as he crawled inside a bottle of the meanest
Mexican spirits.

Careful Skeptic

A close friend once called me
a careful skeptic. Miracles don't come
from eggs, I might say, chickens do.
One morning I talked to a young man
who had broken up with the mother of his child;
He cried about not seeing the baby
and the loss of equilibrium
forced by his confusion.
More than forty years of life
have given me some place in this space.
So we talked about dignity, of the values that
keep one strong when everything else falls apart;
He listened, began to smile, said he would try,
and left, paying for breakfast.
I'm sure he wished an angel
would stride with him through the windswept road.
I don't know about angels; I do know
the miracle germinating at any crossroads
is what's learned.

Woman on the First Street Bridge

Traffic crawled for miles in front of me
and a similar number of miles behind.
Sandwiched between a truck-bed piled
with oil-soaked auto parts and a crumpled sedan,
I felt like melting beneath the peppered sun
as I inhaled the fetid fumes, scratched
my steaming eyeballs, and crept toward
the concrete bridge facing the jagged skyline.
I had been on a work prowl, hiking up and down
factory row next to the housing projects
that lined the east side of the Los Angeles River.
I passed soot-stained brick walls and opened
creaky warehouse doors that sang a chorus
of "no work today" as heartbreaking
as a woman's rejections.

For hours I closed in on secretaries,
bored to their toes, and filled out applications
that were later piled on top of hundreds
with names and personal statistics similar to mine.
Finally, too tired to continue, I sank into my car seat
and entered the crest of blaring vehicles,
feeling like a coffin sliding toward a crematory furnace.

The sun's rays beat malicious against the car's metal top.
Sweat simmered on skin. My breath rose in short gasps.
Then something happened that was as refreshing
as a Tecate beer in the Death Valley desert:
A woman,
who stood at the entrance
of the First Street bridge,
lifted her dress to her neck,

revealing dark nipples on a mass of breasts,
and masturbated to an open-mouthed
audience of imprisoned procession.

She must have known what we were going through;
she must have known what sorcery
could snap us out of it.

Echo Park

Echo Park smiles as summers swarm
over stucco-brown apartments
beaded like sweat. Lonely travelers
step out of the torn-screen doors
of the Paradise Motel and ride.

Carnival lights on a mud lot
beckon the street crawlers. The
amusements reach up to the sky
with colors splashing across the
night's palette in a silent brush.

Winitos crowd the entrances
of the 24-hour Pioneer
Market, their crusted hands open
for change. Darla, *la fea*, accepts
change for back-of-the-alley favors.

Echo Park's playground swells with children
who scramble around the swings,
and they swing and swing
while mothers on chipped benches
relate the nights and indecisions.

I've screamed here, made love here.
I've raced through the shadow of trees,
while *locos* stalked in the damp.
I've cried and laughed here—I once
held my daughter here who fell from the
monkey bars when I wasn't looking.

The lush of Echo Park calls to me.
Waits for me. Tells me lies.
And I believe them. Oh, take me back,
Echo Park, merciless & naughty,
back to the dawn of guitar strings
and strained voices out of yawning windows.

Red Screams

(after a talk with Michael Meade)

The girl who used razors
to slash the length of her arms
called the opened flesh "red screams."
They are the mouths
of all our silences,
for what we can only imagine.
They are the vowels
in octave spiral
toward our fears.
Listening is not enough.
What bass fluctuates in
the resounding pangs
between these ears?
If we get near
let the rhythm speak,
convulsing beneath our caresses.
We may not understand
but I think about this:
if violins could stay our hands,
we'd all learn to play.

The Facts of Life

(To President Bill Clinton on his inaugural January 1993)

Let me tell you the facts of life
   from beneath the tattered coat of my country.
This country whose soul
   has died long before the body.
This country which is blurry eyed
   from lack of dreaming yet full of sleep.
This country which is inebriated
   with guilt and false grinning.
This country which is a beggar's song
   slithering through city veins.
This country which is night spewing
   over the crevices on the face of day.
This country of laughter & illumination
   across the ocean of lies where we drown.
This country of winter's breath
   gusting across a swollen star-spangled sky.
This country which dances without a beat
   in constant searching, constant rupturing.
This country which seethes, that is hungry,
   and limps with ambiguity.
This country satiated with sweet odors & colors,
   yet stenched & scrawled with race hatred.
This country where the road from Hope to hope
   must pass beyond expectation, beyond class privilege.
This country whose penitence is waiting
   at the corner of Fury & Fire.
This country where every promise must be rendered,
   every dream made flesh.
This country where all that's left is to act,
   and my country will act if you won't.

To the Hills of Dirt and Granite

To the Hills of dirt and granite
with roosters preparing for the pits.
The old walls are gone as are the reticent
fields of car parts and grizzled furniture.
Gone is the dread climbing between
lightness and midnight.
How to wipe away the secrets & stains?
How to say we could have saved you
when we didn't?
I'm back and the same sun rains
on the markers in the sea of grass below.
How to return what we have taken?
Where is the voice & timbre to tell the story?
Bodies are pulled through the cracks
of a ground rife with conflict
as we stand on the precipice
of eternal circles.
Memories swim in the matrix
where heart and mind
reverberate in tension.
They implode into incantation.
They churn out snips of verse & prophecy.
They descend as free-falling echoes.
There is no shielding the face of ardor.
There is no hiding in the dark.
I ascend the twisted tree of solace,
along the jointed branches,
sliding my hand over shriveled bark:
Cut from it this pillar of whispers,
wrench out the rumors from these knotted pores.
Tell me, again, the story.

Hungry

My wife left me, taking the two kids
and everything but a few dishes.
Later in this squalid hour
I began an affair
with my wife's best friend.
But she already had three kids and no man
and talked about love and marriage
and I didn't know how to get out of it,
being also too much in need of drink.
Soon I couldn't pay the rent
so I kept getting notices in death tones
about broken bones or whatever.
My friend Franco helped sneak me
out of the place.
Franco and me arrived in the middle of the night
and loaded what little I had onto a pickup truck.
I would come back on other nights to get the mail.
And the woman, who was alone with three kids
and looking for a husband,
kept leaving notes,
and I kept throwing them away.
But the hunger had just begun.
My only property of value then
was a 1954 red Chevy in mint condition.
It had the original skirts,
whitewalls, and chrome hood ornament.
What a prize!
I never wanted to part with it
even as layoff slips and parking tickets
accumulated on the dashboard,
even when I found myself living with Mom and Dad
and the '54 Chevy got stashed out in back.

But the hunger and the drinking
and "looking for love in all the wrong faces"
blurred into a sort of blindness.
I stared out the back window
at that red Chevy
and thought how it resembled a large steak
with egg yolks for headlights.
No, man, I couldn't do it;
I couldn't turn my back on it now.
The days shriveled away
and again I looked out that window
with Mama yelling behind me
about getting a job
and I could taste that last scotch,
that last *carnitas burrito*,
and perhaps take in the stale scent
of a one-room apartment somewhere.
Then the hunger became a fever,
the fever a pain in my head.
And as soon as some dude with 200 bucks came along,
I sold it. God almighty,
I sold my red Chevy!
For 200 bucks!
For nothing, man.
Oh, I thought this would get rid of
my wife's face
in every reflection,
her friend's staring out of my coffee cup,
I thought this would hold me
for more than a week
and end the curses
ringing in my ears.
I sold it! My red Chevy.
Prized possession.
200 bucks.

A Fence of Lights

A row of lights on asphalt
serves as fence between two buildings
separating them
keeping them on their margins of space
the fence gropes in symmetry
as snowflakes descend
like an obscure whiteness dancing
lightly before my gaze
everything is clouded in a density
of winter-screen
as in a memory or painting
while impressions saunter through
as this unfocusing allows me to see
something else about light
about colors
about structure
how the weather is tied to what I see
how what I see is pushing out what I feel
how what I feel becomes what matters
not the flakes, not the row of lights
like fences, not this gravel walk
but the inescapable light-dance of senses

"Eva sitting on the curb with pen and paper before the torturers came to get her"

(a conversation with P.Z.)

The phone call came on a night of a bruising
battle with my computer, writhing out some
scalding word-art. It was from a man who
claimed to be the "King of Poetry."
His first words were: "Are you beauty who
wants to be true?"—and I thought, sure, why not?
People have said worse.
"I am king because I understand
eternal harmony with infinite beauty,"
he continued. And who was I to argue?
"Truth cannot be against the lie; the lie
is against the truth." I was with him so far.
Then he spoke about Eva, a perfect
poet, he claimed, "an angel born for it,"
and how she was "incarnate ecstasy,
light of the absolute." He kept on
with reminiscences, fragments,
and epiphanies, including one about
a seven-year-old Mexican girl
he spotted from a fire escape in Pilsen:
"They will kill her before she is 17,"
he declared. And I agreed: this too is true.
He talked about writing a book for the
universal child, how he had eclipsed
his Italian background to be human,
and how those youth in jail "love death to be
with the dead ones who can't hurt them."
He appeared to surpass even this,
the real, the cold, the brutal

tongues licking us to sleep. Here was a Dante
for our times, whose mythical Eva
rouses poetry from its quilted slumber.
Here was a concrete Buddha, challenging
even me to drink from the chalice of my own gifts.
"You are on your knees—stand up!" he yelled
before hanging up, his words like wings to cross
the battered skies of all illiteracies.

The Old Woman of Mérida

The old woman stares out an open window;
shards of sunlight pierce her face
cutting shadows on skin. She's washing
her hands after the dishes, dipping them
into a sea of hues and shapes,
a sea of syllables without sound,
in a stone house in Mérida,
her Mérida of dense Mexico.

The water is a view to a distant place:
Kitchen walls fall to reveal a gray sky,
an array of birds in flight through fog
—the crushed white of waves curling at feet.
There appears a woman in forested hair,
eyes of black pearl,
who touches the hewn face of a man
and palms that feel like bark.
She cringes at its blemishes
and something in her careens
against the walls of her heart.
She never wants to let go,
never wants to stop tracing
the scars above his eyebrows,
the tattoos on blackened skin,
while the lick of a tongue
stirs the night inside her.

The old woman looks at water and into
this vision shaped into a mouth
—the mouth of the sea that swallowed
her sailor-husband
so many sunlit windows ago.

The Rabbi & the Cholo

The Rabbi appeared, black dressed and uncertain,
like a shadow of doubt. My world
then was perfectly squared: I was at war
with humanity, the Rabbi indistinguishable
from the enemy. I had the world
between my teeth,
gouging at betrayed skies,
seeking deliverance in mortar and brick,
behind tattered sneers.
I shifted the firmament
through thick fingers,
dust in the grooves of skin,
between eyes,
between sighs.

The Rabbi's words broke through
hatred's mask, peeling into
something calm, soft.
He spoke for the centuries:
Of nomadic sons, Hebrew invocations,
desert songs and tattooed numbers.
The Rabbi carried everything for everybody.
He said he feared me, that he had to know me.
His fear and my hate somehow
found fugue and notation,
music and reverberation.

Rabbi and Cholo—the distance as great
as those between L.A. settlements,
different countries really.
He listened to my stories
like a voyeur of myths: stories of scaled fences,

of stray gunfire between blemished palm trees,
of failed robberies and failed courage,
of carnal intimacies with women
dark as me, risking all for the voice
to wrap the flesh like perpetual rain.
The Rabbi and the Cholo. We strolled
the callused streets, across ravines and hills,
through back roads of mud
and rotting cars, places he never knew,
taking in the stinging odors
of urine stains on stucco walls,
of *carnitas* at midnight stalls,
of bloodied roosters in cages
and love-drunk men groping at running ballads
lamenting loss between shots
of earth-born tequila.

I waded through Fairfax corridors,
through hatted men in ancient
arguments, through bagel shops and Synagogue
doorways, dazed at the Mediterranean
gazes of girls and their well-dressed
Brentwood mothers. I stood there
in starched baggy Khaki pants and Pendelton
flannel shirt, buttoned only at the top,
with bandanna and skull cap above my eyes,
among the bearded Semite faces
in black pants and suits, who appeared
like 1920s Lower East Side
or Boyle Heights: Nothing here
but escape,
exile and escape.

One night, at a "brotherhood" camp, the Rabbi
witnessed me break down, for the first time
since I was eleven: I mourned for all
the dead homeys, for the women who walked,
for family and the wounds of silence.
The Rabbi sat down next to me and said:
"I don't know how to cry like that."

The Rabbi and the Cholo:
There is no closing of parting waters here.
I was laughter and sun, vessel
of swollen tales, someone who could shout
when enough is never enough:
My inner-life was close to the touch;
the Rabbi had his layered beneath
charcoal cloth, tradition, voices;
plea and birthright.

One summer we gazed at the ocean
that caressed Venice Beach.
I focused on the waves,
the froth, the wreckage of sea;
the Rabbi took in the deep lull
and blue mass at the distance.
In a hasty moment, on that sodden shore,
severed from history, I responded
as if "this too will pass."
The issues were immediate, my enemies close,
nothing vast like time:
My grief was simple then, pure,
definite—now.
The Rabbi was nothing if not history,
time for him an immense divide:
his grief, forever.

¡*Yo Voy Ami!*

(For Arlene Osuna and the people of Humboldt Park)

Tuck-pointed brick scrapes up against dead branches with
    weathered gray backstairs and alleys scrawled with breath;

these are nights of girls shrieking, of drunken men in
    muddled Spanish, pulling women out of their depths;

these are nights of young couples, newly-wed poor,
    threatening to pay rent while an eruption of semi-

automatics welcomes them and Toyota hatchbacks
    cruise by with large speakers out the back, thumping Street

Mixes, and decals of *"Yo Voy Ami"* and *"Soy
    Boricua"* on their windows. *Así y asá.*

Tri-colored flags are sold at the edge of *el parque*
    Humboldt next to Pentecostals enticing sinners

and housewives to open-air tents while a live band
    jump-starts the vibes in their chests and peddlers prepare

mofongo and *piraguas* for the shift-changing
    gente de trabajo; children race ahead of their

mothers who are busy *averiguando la mortificación*
    of life to neighbors with homemade *pasteles*

in paper sacks; police detour traffic for summer
    block parties as fire hydrants with inner tubes wrapped

around the openings blast relief to the shorties
    browning beneath a searing sun; nearby, my teenage

neighbor, with a prosthetic foot after the real
    one had been accidentally shot off when she

was three, calls over thirteen-year-old Arlene,
    who sometimes watches over my one-year-old son,

who's barely able to walk yet is fast when one
    isn't looking. *Así y asá.* Two years later Arlene

is killed when a bullet meant for her boyfriend claims
    her instead. Mingo next door has chickens and roosters

in the backyard. He dreams of Ponce in its breezes
    yet lures part of the island to Mozart Street.

My Jamaican neighbor also yearns for Caribbean
    waters, but his Alabama-born wife only

misses the open spaces of her home; some time
    later we see their sons in the juvenile

court when my oldest boy has a hearing at the
    same time. One day a coffee-colored dove lands

on my head outside my front door. It ambles to my
    shoulder and stays there. I end up getting a cage

and keeping it for a few days until the constant
    cooing and spurts of dove wails grate on my nerves.

I finally had it with the bird when my wife
    and I almost come to blows over whether we should

cover the cage to keep it quiet. I give the damn
    thing to Mingo. On hot weekends, neighbors aim

speakers out their windows while others then push out
    their own sounds and the competing *salsa* permeates

the street while local drug dealers appear with school-age
    boys as look-outs. After a while, I don't mind the

racket outside, but just don't have a faucet leak
    in the kitchen or I go nuts. *Así y asá.*

Oh Arlene, sweet Arlene, with straight burnished hair and
    luminous eyes, with wisps of girl legs and morning

sacraments of smile, framed by wrought iron fences.
    Bendita, you deserved more than this world would give!

Fire

(for Eduardo Galeano)

1.

It seems our days are shaped by conflagration.
Felice, a poet from Chicago, recalls
the sugar canes of Santo Domingo—
black acrid taste in the Caribbean sun.

I remember Oaxaca where flames swirled
around a row of severed steer heads, eyes boiling,
as an Indian hand tears off
muscle and meat for tacos.

And then also Managua where tires
kindle, arousing an odor akin to acid,
to protest Contra raids
or another injustice.

African drums. Indigenous flutes.
Gypsies and a deep song.
Their rhythms rise like steam,
fueled by an earth *elumbrada*.

Fire follows us like family,
like the rivers of revolt
in San Salvador, Leon and Chiapas,
forever traced in mind.

2.

In Chicago, depressed neighborhoods
are dotted with vacant lots like missing
teeth in an old man's mouth as buildings
are torched for insurance claims.

Consuming blaze once stormed through a three-flat
in the *barrio* of Pilsen.
Men, women & children poured out doors,
jumped out windows, some with clothes clinging on flesh.

They accounted for all the occupants except
a 12-year-old boy; a father paced frantic
as firefighters drenched a collapsing roof.
For three days crews scoured the scorch.

Neighbors held a vigil as soaked and charred
walls crumbled in the search. And every
morning the alderman waited outside,
his own little girl in arms.

When finally city workers pulled
the boy out of the ruins, hundreds hushed
as he appeared among them, this *mestizaje*
devoured by the hell-spawn that never ceases

to stir us, to smolder in our breasts,
as fire becomes the luminous dawn,
the squeeze of skin, this memory
called our history.

To the police officer who refused to
sit in the same room as my son because
he's a "gang banger":

How dare you!
How dare you pull this mantle from your sloven
sleeve and think it worthy enough to cover my boy.
How dare you judge when you also wallow in this mud.
Society has turned over its power to you,
relinquishing its rule, turned it over
to the man in the mask, whose face never changes,
always distorts, who does not live where I live,
but commands the corners, who does not have to await
the nightmares, the street chants, the bullets,
the early-morning calls, but looks over at us
and demeans, calls us animals, not worthy
of his presence, and I have to say: How dare you!
My son deserves to live as all young people.
He deserves a future and a job. He deserves
contemplation. I can't turn away as you.
Yet you govern us? Hear my son's talk.
Hear his plea within his pronouncement,
his cry between the breach of his hard words.
My son speaks in two voices, one of a boy,
the other of a man. One is breaking through,
the other just hangs. Listen, you who can turn away,
who can make such a choice; you who have sons
of your own, but do not hear them!
My son has a face too dark, features too foreign,
a tongue too tangled, yet he reveals, he truths,
he sings your demented rage, but he sings.
You have nothing to rage because it is outside of you.
He is inside of me. His horror is mine. I see what
he sees. And if my son dreams, if he plays, if he smirks

in the mist of moon-glow, there I will be, smiling
through the blackened, cluttered and snarling pathway
toward your wilted heart.

The Quiet Woman

The quiet woman roams in the din of belly screams.
She knows rivers and caves and curbsides.
She knows the advent of furled fists.
She is the quiet woman, shadow on park bench,
pushed into needle grass, a disheveled syllable
uttered between makeshift schemes. The burden
of memories is the salvage of fantasy flames,
the mossed-faced whose stare streams through stria.
Here comes the quiet woman, a blossom in the wound
of night. The miracle-pulp in her hands. She swerves
around odors of hurt, odors of neglect,
of treachery and a lie. What's the scent of a poem?
The quiet woman knows; she breathes it in
and exhales. Others take the natural away,
remove the tender. All that's left is facade
and caricature. All veneer and word play.
But for a quiet woman, a poem is a smile so open
she's afraid of falling in.

Markets, Alleys & the Hounds of Hell

My brother, whom we called Rano,
never liked playing with me.
But if he had to, mostly because
of the striking hand of my mother,
he would terrorize me with small tortures.
One time Mama asked my brother
to go to the market and pick up a few items.
"And take *el grillo pelón* with you," she yelled.
For most of my childhood, I was known as
el grillo pelón—the bald cricket—after Mama
kept my hair shorn to help keep the lice out.
"Oh, man, do I have to?" Rano responded.
"*¿Cómo que no?* He's your brother."
As if this would move him to say,
"Of course, this is why I should treat him
with great care and concern."
Yeah, right! Not Rano.
What I learned about my brother
was that nothing he did or suggested
had anything innocent or safe about it.
Case in point: after we bought a few items
and managed to make it out of the store,
he showed me the candy he had absconded
with from the checkstand.
Still I always fell for whatever scraps
of kindness he'd throw my way;
when he offered to put me inside
the market cart and push
—I was four years old to his seven—
I jumped on this. So off we go,
down the scrawled banks of a sewer wash,
through dry foliage, and then up a sidewalkless
street. It started to become fun.
Rano maneuvered the cart around broken bottles

and sinkholes while I took in the sights,
enjoying them for once since most of the time
I stepped into this terrain,
I'd get chased by older boys.
Rano turned into a dirt alley,
and we kept going, merrily along,
looking into many a forlorn backyard,
many a sad shed and pathetic garage.
Then, in a whirlwind of fury,
three monstrous, massive, mammoth
(adjectives escape me)
Great Danes came at us from the side
of a wood-shingled house,
rushing like steeds,
toward the back fence!
Rano stopped dead in his tracks;
I almost fell over the front end of the cart.
You'd think he'd turn the contraption around
and scurry me to safety.
But did I say I knew my brother!
Sure enough, as if by impulse, as the dogs'
fangs tore at sections of the fence,
Rano shoved the market cart and its precious
cargo, including the groceries (not even these
warranted much favor with Rano)
toward the death jaws in brown jowls.
I screamed through my eye sockets.
My arms in an uncontrollable frenzy above me.
Panic gripping me from the bandages on my shins
to the lice on my head.
Fortunately, the dogs stayed behind
their side of the fence,
barking spittle and teeth into my face.
I spun around to see Rano
several yards into the alley
inflamed with laughter.

The Feathered Warrior

*(for Marcos Cordova, who at 16 years old was
killed in the streets of Chicago)*

The streets call out many
to be renamed,
to be initiated
into a world,
to be reborn into darkness,
to taste death so as to revel in it;
streets that feed off
all the great hungers,
all the great angers.
These streets have called out a fine warrior,
who fought with fire and feathers,
who ran poetic fingers over concrete
walks—a warrior who carried
the rage for all of us,
pushing the emotional edges
to the depths of all our rivers.
He scared the world with honesty
because justice ran in his veins
as did the street's blood.
His death has given us life,
not as savior, but as our son,
who has toppled the betraying fathers.
Clay, feathers and jade eyes:
Sixteen years of man madness
created such a dreamer.

Cloth of Muscle and Hair

Pink, oily bodies hang on a line
like cloth of muscle and hair.
Flayed in rapid order with a delicate slice
of pelt, they are held by their feet, their skin
pulled from the flesh, down toward the damp
ground. The five-year-old girl wept, having held
these same rabbits only a day before,
gathering them close, fur to face, stroking them
and sensing their pulse beneath her fingers.
My Greek neighbor had done this for years,
raising rabbits to die, and displaying them
on a nylon wire to sell to other neighbors.
The girl's tears failed to spark in him
a gnawing nightmare of wet body parts
lurching through late night foam,
creeping up the back while wailing out
our mortality, proving we are no less
flayable, with emotions ripped
from the muscles of psyche. Nothing
stirred the panic from my neighbor's hand
even as the girl ran into the house,
unable to bear the dead rabbits,
with their furred feet intact,
speaking to her of how soft things can lose
their mild yielding, how they can become
creatures of clawed meat, become objects
that invade wretched memory when something,
anything, pushes out the soft white sheath
of innocence.

Boy of All Boys

(To Ramiro)

The 10-year-old child
hopped a freight train
departing from Los Angeles
to Chicago.

Police pulled him out
of the boxcar just before
it left the city.
He said he was going
to see his father:
he had missed the voice.

To me he was the smile of a boy;
the boy of all boys.
I only recalled the good times,
like when I took him to the park,
rented a boat and watched as he
maneuvered it toward the wading ducks.
I failed to sense the despair.
It came in a midnight phone call.
It came in the demands for fatherhood.
It came as I began a new family.

The boy never wanted me to forget.
He never wanted the hearts to stop
beating between us.
He hopped a train.
He sought my voice.
I only recalled the good times.

Poem for Shakespeare & Company

*(for George Whitman and his great book store in
Paris on the occasion of a fire, July 18, 1990, which
destroyed much of the store's Sylvia Beach Library)*

There is a burnt room
above the Shakespeare & Co. bookstore:
A library once full of books
now ash. It speaks of how
books burn so well:
the pulp and cloth ablaze
like great forest fires.
But George Whitman knows
books burn bright without flame.
Every voice at Shakespeare and Company
is the hum of minds ablaze in books.
And Whitman has books to kill for.

At the Tumbleweed Hotel
there are books and faces on every wall.
There are photos of Whitman
with the fiery eyes of revolution.
These are books and faces
that are humanity's
hobbled steps toward heaven.
Here words swirl around me
as fire does around a book.
And I know: I am
the pulp and cloth these walls
were meant to engulf.

Rant, Rave & Ricochet

Police killed her brother
for stealing a piece of chicken;

she says there's nothing
to do but squat. She's had

babies this way. Some nothing
more than arteries,

gray matter and fluid.
Three came out all right,

and were taken away
by bureaucrats. She's homeless.

She's been raped and almost killed.
They say she's mad. For her,

sanity is a crime.
"I'm not stuck on stupid,"

she exclaims, and welcomes the
chaos which crackles out

of social construct. It's
her only peace in the

piece of the street at war.
She rants & raves, but it's all

ricochet from the bullet
that has claimed her since birth.

She pulls at strands of hair
flooding a furrowed face,

declares herself twine,
thimble and an ace of hearts.

¡Seguro Que Hell Yes!

(apologies to Flaco Jimenez)

We have passed this way before,
laden with sod, skeleton tongues
marking the dark. We have eaten of this
dust, we have scraped it off our faces,
we have dreamed this wound, this world
of vileness *tantas veces* that it's a song
beneath our breathing. *¡Seguro Que Sí!*
We knew it was coming before it came.
Ya hemos pasado por este camino,
and venom eyes seek us, taunting
mouths greet us. The most rooted people
of the land are the most revered
and the most despised, making us myths
even as mother earth daily births us.
We cross many borders and cross
into ourselves. This America
that Emerson called a poem
is a barbed wire. Our sweat, our blood,
and the *lagrimas* shed for thee,
are fashioned into a prison.
Freedom for some is slavery for me.
Whenever they lie, a part of us
is murdered. This we know, and our
children cannot let it be. This we know,
and we challenge our skins to take it on.
This we know because we have passed
this way before, *sequro que sí*, cactus
bedding at our feet, snake curling through
our limbs. *Ya hemos pasado por este camino,*
and we can never stop coming.

49

The desert calls us: the fire-scarred trees,
the dried bones of elders, the silent screaming
of stones, they call us back
and we come, because we have died so many
times to the sun, because we belong
to the rivers wild, because
we never feared the blue
in the eye, the green in the heart,
the searing laws and guns and lies,
because we dreamed all this,
and now we are awake to dream again.
¡*Seguro que* hell yes!

Women the Color of Newspaper

(for Wanda, Barbara, Eileen and Margaret,
whose words are embedded in this poem)

They are women the color of newspaper
with seething sentences seesawing line for line:
this phrase is a life, this stanza a story
—fever to fill the tributaries of tombs.

Metaphors to munch on, meter to matter.
Similes are a swollen smile, coffee
becomes chatter. Barbara's poetry is sculpture.
Wanda is a pen in flight.
Eileen's verses are her children;
Margaret's are pure light.

They carry a multitude of deterred faces,
writing with their spines.
They are women the color of newspaper,
lusting between shelter walls,
with gossip for the thirst of ears
and poems enough to braid.

Night Shift at St. Regis

I worked several months at the St. Regis
Paper Company as a "utility man."
My job was to move immense rolls of paper,
cut their steel wrappings with tools
that resembled car theft equipment (more on this
later) and attach them to the back of paper-bag
making machines, usually run by women,
with hefty guys as bag catchers on the other end.
A 24-hour operation, I started in the graveyard
shift. My fellow operatives were usually
African and Mexican, with a *güero* face here and there.
My *compadre* Tony also worked at St. Regis.
A Jewish-Italian who once lived in the
mostly Mexican-and-Black Aliso Village
Housing Projects in East L.A.,
Tony was sometimes more Chicano in manner
than some Chicanos I knew,
but he also had this kind of brash,
take-care-of-business, I-know-what-I'm-
talking-about "white guy" demeanor;
still he was my best friend, my *compa*,
and we tried never to let each other down.
Me and my other partners—including Paul,
the Fremont High School drop-out from South
Central L.A., and Leo, the Hopi-Laguna homeboy
who lived in the Pico Gardens Housing Projects—
were this multi-national crew
of young revolutionaries, taking on schools,
capitalists, sell-outs, boot-lickers,
and neo-nazi-white-supremacists,
(we loved the fight, good or otherwise);
Being employed at St. Regis
was how we handed ourselves over to the world.

To stay awake on those God-awful hours,
I slept during the day in the makeshift bombshelter
that my future mother-in-law had built
in her City Terrace backyard.
She believed the *comunistas* were going
to drop the bomb any day—and she was ready.
Truth be told, it probably couldn't survive a minor
fireworks display, but the place was great for sleeping
since it was dark, burrowed deep, and I didn't need
to place aluminum foil on any windows.
I would arrive to work near the midnight hour,
tools in hand, and step into the din
of the gigantic machinery, punching in on
a time clock, and falling into place as the
previous shifts' utility man groggily left the mill floor.

The work required the same gestures, the same
dance every night, hauling rolled paper taller than me
into alignment behind machines that
cranked out thousands of paper bags per shift.
Sometimes, I'd get so damn beat
that my motions became like in a dream
and my eyelids descended against my will.
Once I fell asleep standing up
—and almost toppled into a machine's gearworks!
But I couldn't rest until the designated breaks.
And the dance continued
until dawn broke through the shattered
glass of the overhead windows near the corrugated tin roof.
One morning, as I tottered to my car in the parking lot,
a police car pulled up behind me.
"Hold it right there, buddy!" an officer exclaimed
while climbing out of the car.
Carajo, it had been a while since police had snuck up
on me. And although I now was a crime-free working stiff,

I apparently still had the "criminal" stain.
"What you got in your hands?" another officer
barked, as he merged right from his partner's left.
"These are my work tools," I replied,
too weary to get too agitated.
"Yeah, what kind of work—stealing cars?" he blurted out.
"No, I'm over at St. Regis; if you like, we can walk over
and talk to the foreman."
Great idea. It should've worked. But not before they
forced my hands over the car's hood,
had me open my car with the keys, and threatened
to take me in when I tried to further explain myself.
But I held my own, maintaining
my innocence while remaining calm, even after
the officers claimed there were many car thefts in the area
and that my tools were similar to those belonging
to a thief (actually car theft tools, such as a jimmy bar,
looked nothing like my "utility man" chisel and steel
hammer. But I supposed they were close).
Finally, when my request to check my job status sank in,
the officers backed off.
I also began to look more liked a tired,
overworked, and quite legit young employee
who was planning to get married in a couple of months.
"Okay, we'll let you go for now (thanks for the favor),
but whoever is stealing these cars will be caught!"
(Adam 12, where are you when we need you?)

St. Regis offered no perks and little advancement
except perhaps to become a utility man on the
afternoon turn. But I gave it my all. Sometimes,
I actually liked being there; something about
the rhythms, the lateness of hour, the way the day
crowds out the night and the sun climbs up
on the sky in slow, calculated steps.

Then, just before my six-month's probation period
ended, I got called into Johnny Brown's office;
he was the plant's graveyard supervisor.
"Sit down, young man," he said, not looking up.
"I've been watching your performance
for some time now. I must say, I see much lacking
in your speed, much lacking in desire."
I had no idea what he was talking about.
"If you want to remain on this job, you'll have to
pick up the pace. You're slowing down the whole
production. You have to catch up. There's
much at stake here. We can't afford any
loss time. You want a future with St. Regis,
you have to sharpen up, get on the stick,
put your best foot forward. Understand?"
Sure, but this didn't seem to correspond
to what I was doing. For a second,
I thought maybe he had me confused, but no—
it was my personnel file in front of his face!
As I left his office, I felt devastated:
I had heaved a lot of energy into the job,
and still I didn't seem to make the grade.
Johnny Brown spoke in a tedious tone,
but it was authoritative and final.
I thought for sure I wouldn't make my probation,
that I'd probably have to call off the wedding,
because without a job, what kind of home
could I provide my bride!
I walked out that day with my stomach
in knots; I couldn't even knock out as usual.
I called Tony to tell him I wasn't going to make it at St. Regis.
Tony listened intently, an obese silence
on the other end of the line.
Then, in the same banal voice as Johnny Brown's,
he repeated word for word what the man had told me.

Hey? How did you know what he said?
"That's Johnny Brown," Tony assured.
"He says the same thing to everybody
who's near their end of probation. You're all right.
If you were really that bad, he would've fired you."
Well, I don't appreciate this at all.
"I know, it stinks," Tony continued. "But that's his way
of keeping the new employees under his thumb.
For people like Johnny Brown, you'll never be
good enough! He's just a hack.
He's never done the work you're doing.
Don't worry about it."
Oh.

I stayed on at St. Regis a few more months
and eventually did get hitched.
I also stopped getting pestered by police
in the parking lot.
And I got used to the graveyard shift,
when the darkness swam easily in my bones,
the vampire came out,
and the bloodlust overwhelmed me (just kidding).
On top of this, I learned to trundle the paper
as fast as anyone at the plant,
which is nothing to sniff at, let me tell you,
when one works at St. Regis.

Reflection on El Train Glass

Gaze penetrates through the glass
of El train window. It infringes
& infiltrates, a misdemeanor
against silence. I turn toward it.
The face in the haze refracting glare
in myriad directions; slicing into
working woman's tiredness, into
child's affront, into uniformed
man's wariness, into the uninterested
below city still-life.

A vise of sun rays grips a shape,
an innuendo of myself.
A caress of shade on the cheek.
I'm recalling the places I've been,
like flesh below the waters of a bath,
and I sleep into this transparent
world, sleep into a sort of flying,
into molds of day, into cinders
and the feel which doesn't feel, into
a stupor deeper than reflection.

Rocks

Diana has a *tapiz* with sewn rocks
she calls "intifada." Rocks come
in course edges; the better to slice,
the better to leave marks, to feel
the hate that bombs only wipe away.

There were rocks in Juchitan as natives
of this Zapoteca country defended
their hold of the municipal palace,
a protest to Mexico's ruling party's
"dictacracy." Rocks hurt.

My *compadre* says he'd rather be in a gunfight
than one with rocks.

There were rocks in Overton when a court
freed a cop who killed an Overton mother's
son. A boulder from a freeway overpass
almost struck a businessman who happened
to pass through the O on his way home.

There were rocks in Watts, flaming spears
hurled into the mouth of America's shame.
Nat Brown was there (life-long Watts resident).
When tourists came after the squelching,
he sold them rocks from the railroad tracks.

Nat claimed they were the first ones thrown,
and everyone was buying.

Freeway Flyin' Burrito Man

Shannon had these friends: burly, oil-smeared,
leather-and-denim tattooed bikers
who stopped by the house and wondered how
this lowrider-cum-writer could end up living
with their Country & Western loving,
tall blond, daisy-duke-wearing cowgirl.
This didn't bother me none. But I knew
they couldn't deal with it.
One day, on my way out of the California desert
to visit L.A., one of her friends offered
to take me to the bus station. Cool.
I climbed onto the back of his chopper
just before the dude ripped up the street
to the nearest freeway.
He turned into the entrance
at 60 miles per hour, then proceeded
to rack up speeds of up to 90
while I held on with white knuckles;
my hair flew in the wind
as did my stomach muscles.
He got off the freeway the same way
he got on. He roared through
over-turned train tracks and beaten-down roads
into the Greyhound station, screeching to a halt.
How we arrived in one piece, I'll never know.
I jumped off the hog and then faced the biker.
He also dismounted and glared at me
like he was going to whack me in the mouth.
But I stood there, my body solid with adrenaline,
my brows scowled. My eyes mad-dogging.
We stood there for a long time,
without saying a word.

Suddenly he backed off, vaulted onto the bike,
and sped off with dust settling about my feet.
I knew he wanted to scare the crap
out of me; he probably hoped
to knock me down but wasn't sure
if I could hold my own.
This was his mistake.
When I returned to my desert home,
I told Shannon her friends were no longer
welcome—and if she didn't like this,
she could follow them out as well.
"He had his chance, and he blew it," I said
"He'll never get that chance again."
He never did. Shannon stayed.

Questions for Which You Are Always the Answer

(for Maria Trinidad, "La Trini")

Whose Jalisco harangues the Jalisco in my stroll;
who lays across the ruins of Teotihuacan like rainwater;
whose face outlines the bathroom walls of *cantinas*;
who is the *aguardiente* that tongues my callused throat?
What sleep becomes the dexterous hand of memory;
what skin is the lodestone of desire;
what song is fusion between a woman's walk and sunrise;
what drunkenness befalls while falling into those native eyes;
what stitching collects the shreds of midnight silence?
Who says what only solace can say,
what only mariachi's horns and good mescal can vanquish?
What bones lift this face to a face of lovely bones;
what moist fingers straightens the collars of qualms;
what evening wind arouses the color in blood,
pretending the wet in water;
what voice is chocolate icing?
How deep are the potholes of lust;
how necessary is the milk of that touch;
how perpetual is the distance of thighs;
how vaginal is the soul's vortex?
Trini, you know what I can't know:
what tempest gathers in my lungs.

Rainfall Piano

"I wish I could swallow music,
fill myself with drumbeats and rainfall piano."
—Patricia Smith

Filo walked out my front door,
made it to the corner
and got shot.
When I saw him at the hospital,
he looked up from the gurney,
bottles of fluid attached to his arms,
and grinned.
When Papo got hit three times with a .44
we thought he wouldn't make it.
He lost part of a finger
and still limps;
now he's serving 40 years
at Stateville
accused of exacting revenge
on one of the dudes
who laughed at him.
I can hardly listen to music anymore,
to Patricia's rainfall piano
playing the keys of desire on a CD.
The gunfire is louder.
Recently somebody sprayed
the pre-kindergarten graduation
ceremony at the elementary school
down my street.
Nobody got hit.
The parents stood there
dumbfounded;
the children instantly
dropped to the ground.

Civilization

"I am tired of building up somebody else's civilization"
—Fenton Johnson

There are days when sunshine is toxic, when breathing
becomes fatal and the love stares of innocence have fangs.
There are days when caresses are lethal drumming
and the low murmur of a child's voice is a hand slap
of hell flames across my face; when all civilization is a squabble
in my partner's gaze and morality is a gun at my head.
I didn't make this place. So what if I say you can eat it! Eat it
and choke. This heart-a-choke, this diet of hypocrisies,
this horse feed of fed horses. This salt seasoning
all wounds. Tear it down! Then wake me up when it's over.
Should I care if you don't care? Should I sweat the details when
the whole *enchilada* reeks? Just because you wear a hat and call
that fashion? Because you love the prison and hate the alien?
Don't come to me whining about your lost glories—
they are the lashes on slave skin, the gold stolen off the blanket
of stones called our land; they are the tongues cut
from wiser heads, the deflowered, dehydrated sirens that called
you, then were slaughtered.
Don't cry for me Argentina, or Pennsylvania.
You say I'm no good, but my pathologies
are what's keeping me from cutting your throats.
All enslavers. All exploiters. All engravers of God-money.
You who see my children and go insane,
who wear the flesh of Nahuas like shiny suits,
who have Black Hills in your nightmares,
who eat with Che's severed hands,
who feed your wives to dogs on cracked plates,
who provide heroin to chiseled daughters,
who bathe in the Trail of Tears,
who sell tickets to the Middle Passage,

whose academies hold literature hostage,
whose culture crumbles in the hand
of a glue-sniffing Salvadoran child.

II

Poems Too Short to Braid

Next Generation

There is a death sentence
poised above the boys
who, even now, straddle
the razor edge of living and dying;
And what of the girls?
They try so hard
only to end up as mothers
to the fathers
who mutate the daughters.

Afterbirth

I arrived as afterbirth,
the second child, the one

engorged with nourishment;
I came as appendage

to be scrubbed, probed, picked at
and discarded; I emerged without

wailing, blind, an amphora
of yearning; I had no mouth

but am the feed for all
life, the death-wish for eternity.

At Quenchers Bar When You Said Goodbye

When I sink into your waters,
I only know drowning.
I forget when we started to talk again
as one forgets the first time
one spoke as a child.
But every time we argue
and then get back together
we are like two legs
parting
to give birth.

The Face on the Radio

Helicopters hover like hellish hogs
of Armageddon:
an infra-red shakedown.
We are the enemy, the face on the radio;
burnt petals cluttering the sidewalk.
We are daylight's demise, dancing between
discord & distrust. All is bitter harvest,
betrayal and bewilderment;
all is seed for the fields of retreat:

bullets punctuate every poem.

Tossed-turned Bodies

Tossed-turned bodies deluge the decayed floor;
they hide the hideous within hollowed mores.
Death is but a door they close;
sleep is for sleeping,
the wine they chose.

Every going is coming. Every coming is gone.
They say goodbye once and it's forever;
they're welcomed once
and are always home.

The Object of Intent Is to Get There

"I am in the world to change the world."
—Muriel Rukeyser

One lifetime meets another lifetime
in a constant lifetime of wars.
Leaning cities greet us at every station
and every wound points to the same place.
If your unique pain cancels my unique pain
then there is nothing unique about pain.
What's left to do
but carry your troubles to where they're going;
once there, you stumble on the rest of us.

Messages

A telephone call left a message,
every word like every prayer;
a message of love
serious as a sidewalk.
Where was I?
Too busy writing,
mother language come to feed me,
and failing to leave a message.

Untouched

A tequila bottle is perched
in the pantry, untouched,
next to the vinegar,
a sticky container of corn syrup
& an unopened can of black olives.
Visitation is sweet;
now only the aroma
stings the fingers.

A Father's Lesson

My mother warned
my brother and I
how my father
was going to punish us
for having pictures of nude women
under our mattress.
Anticipation was intense.
Finally, when the *viejo* came home,
he looked at the photos,
gave us a short stern talk,
sent us to our rooms
then calmly
placed the pictures
in his shirt pocket.

Francisca

Untimely visions of you
while driving into a cloud.
All I remember
is jagged glass
and many regrets
balanced across
your glossed lips.

This Could Have Happened

Some guy in red-and-white hooded jacket,
beard in bedraggled dress,
stood on a corner of Chicago's Magnificent Mile
during peak Christmas shopping days
as wet snow drifted about his ears
and the red in his cheeks froze on his face:
In his hands was a sign that read:
Will sell books for food.
And every once in a while he'd look at the sign
as if something were missing,
wondering why nobody
was taking him up on the offer.

Getting Over

A sword to a word
—this is what poetry's about,
crazed with clarity,
held in the prism of an iris,
perpetually pregnant

and getting over.

Suburbia

"Oppression makes even God smell foul."
—Felipe Luciano

Reading the newspaper I feel like an accomplice;
a voyeur is also guilty of something.
So the murders, the corruptions,
and calculated larcenies against the spirit
dwell in me too.
It's easy, I suppose, to pretend
I don't pay rent to the conspiracies.
And that the church is immune
because it's tax exempt.
But from a landfill or cemetery
grow multi-colored flowers.
Who can say then
from what polluted soils
my blossoms will spring?

Believe me when I say . . .

water is the skin of the earth
trains are arteries with corpuscles of people
a sigh is an ancestor praying
a woman's body is suspended over the land
tears come from clouds in your head
writing a poem is like fathering a river
waiting is the art of desire
something about a city makes you want to kill
fetuses scribble on the walls of wombs

III

Notes of a Bald Cricket

Notes of a Bald Cricket

1. I sit alone, a bald cricket, in a bar on "poetry" night, face in a bottle,
singing the amber waves of beer. Poetry is the excuse,
as good as any. Be true to my art. But this is not what keeps
me here: it's the way tequila germinates inside like a gnarled tree,
the way bodies darken into a sort of sunken beauty,
lights low and voices high, the way I can swim between these
back-lit walls. There is death to meet us, swollen hands
to wake us, a life that is falling into the gaps in the floor under our feet.
There are levels of delusions not even churches can attain.
Alchemists straddle bar stools, transformers and transformed,
awaiting my arrival into their webs of splintered stories
while manacled to curled ghosts called gin. I want
to trace the lies on women's skins, to vanish in their wine-drenched
eyes; I want to be flute and whisper, pubic hair and cumshot,
to warrant enough attention so they try to run me over in their cars.
I pause between lingering words, imagining their flight above me,
words to pull into my mouth, to drown into a shot glass,
words of infinite pain, a pain without words; words that claw
at the ceiling, that cough up blood, words that vomit
out of me in back alleys beside rat shit and wet cardboard; words that
slap me silly, that want to rifle through a man's wallet and slip a
hand beneath a woman's skirt; words that eat *tacos de pollo*, with extra-
hot *salsa*, that play muffled trumpet into the reeking streets, words
to drown out the el train rumbling overhead, drowning out my words.
Crying can't speak. Tears only fall into empty palms. Tears & night.
Night becomes the texture of memory, a humid breath glistening
perspiration on my forehead. Wandering from table to table,
my glass held unsteadily in my hand, I stave off hungers
even a double-champ cheeseburger with bacon cannot do.
Hungers for my friend's girlfriend, blue-eyed, dark-haired,
Polynesian-and-Irish, whose fingers I reach out for, whose hair
I want to shampoo, whose body I long to tread upon as if it were

autumn woods or a stretch of beach, with my toes deep into damp sand.
Every smile is a door, every glance a large bed to lay my head, a pillow
of eyelashes to soften the fall. Tequila, *ron*, blue whiskey for a blue
emotion. Mammary glands to memory glands. Each recalling a *deja vu*
of startled intent. There are feels I always want to feel. There are voices
I would rip faded curtains to hear. There are faces to break
chrome-backed glass for, reflections of a liquid stare into millenniums
of stares. I'm dawdling on the edge of this sea in a glass, this last vestige
of my mother's fears, this grandfather poison that poisoned
my grandfather, this nectar of dried screams, this bruised cant,
this woman who presses her nipples to my cheeks, whose chatter
cannot be climbed, whose kisses are stained lullabies, who tells me
I belong although I cannot fit, who dares the fool's lament,
the call and response of night crawlers, the tones beneath my rambling,
who has become the last shriek of tequila dreaming,
whom I now grieve, ambling to the funeral tune of a child's cry
pulsing silent yet determined inside me.
O for beauty's fists to pommel this mask into itself,
for taste that is candy and not porcelain,
for wisps of saliva to wither on my hair and chin,
for words to nuzzle and soak my tongue,
for language's naked prowlness to enter these shoes;
for a bald cricket's lyrical death on a dance floor.

2. The Austrian wall held my shadow, stretched out across ancient wood
that framed my body against the ground. Where was I? People walked
around me, speaking fugues I could not recognize. I felt as if I was going to
die. I hadn't felt this way since I last OD'd on carga so many flights of stairs
ago. I rose from that blessed spot, rose to face the somber street, to wander
among the shadows held by walls, to glimpse my mortality reclining against
a street lamp. My friends were long gone. Sometime the night before, I
wandered off from where we had been gathered: a schnitzel and hot dog
stand near a bar where I had at least 25 of those large, dark and heavy
German beers. This strange place, alien enough to break my hard-found
sobriety, pulled me into its steely grasp, harsh violin music between my

ears, fooling the fool into believing. I numbly went through my pants. In a pocket I found a card with the address to the Salzburg hotel we were staying at. I located a lone taxi and showed the driver the card. I didn't say anything, but whatever expression I gave him told him what he needed to know. He invited me into the cab, then proceeded to take me to the hotel. I paid and tipped the driver, and he pushed off as if all his nights were spent picking up shadows. The next day, we left the hotel to take a train back to Berlin. On the way out, I briefly excused myself from the others, walked to the public restroom in the lobby, and threw up as soon as I opened the door.

In this classroom of crammed heads
I don't want to be seen,
to be called, so I hide.
I want to go back to what I do:
play in my mind. I imagine
all the time, everything.
School. Other kids. They only get in the way.
I'm here because I have to be.
Soon nobody sees me. Nobody calls.
And my head is in scenes.
I'm in the sunlight. I'm on the grass.
I'm voices of battlefields;
I'm the drama of afternoon conflicts
in the dust. I'm a TV screen bursting lines.
I'm airplane crashes. Moonship flights.
I'm raindrops and cascades of flowers
outside every window. I'm running boy.
I'm dog in the alleys of my deeper eye.
I'm a box of space alloy, floating
through the universe.

3. Trini cried when I cried. I couldn't tell her why I went to the recovery program until I had already gone and decided I would stop drinking. I didn't want her to know how bad it had gotten. I didn't want her to see

me, desperate, and then to have her walk out. By rights, she should have. She cried when I cried. Not saying much. Letting my outpouring tell the tale. Letting this say more than what I could have said in letters I wished I had written to all the therapists, to the former wives, to my kids, to confused lovers. Letters I want to compose every night of my life until I expire, letters about the brutal awakening to fire that this sobriety has thrust on me. Trini cried when I cried, as I sat on my office chair in the library of our new home that I knew I could destroy, as other households had been, unless I now opened up, now tasted the salt of Trini's anguish and know she would still be there, as she was then, sliding up to me and placing her arms around my shoulders, and me feeling so ashamed, so bone-hungry, so liquefied soul, so blood-red sorry, and damn-near death tired.

There are moments meant for moments.
Times in which the drowning mattered
more than the woman.
More than sex sometimes.
More than poetry crawling up my spine.
More than my daughter's small hand in mine.
More than water in storms of sand.
More than a map to my scattered past.
More than my son's pleading for play.
More than a mother's small shrill tone on the phone line:
"whatever you do, m'ijo, don't drink."

4. I sprawled on the ground. My back against a small tree trunk. Along a row of white bungalows. On the wet grass of morning. Before open doorways. Faces peering into the blisters of day. My mouth dry as an unopened attic. My clothes in disarray. My eyes partly shut and unable to make out the figures that strolled past me, as in a funeral march, without glancing toward this pile of leaves that maybe looked human as the Las Vegas sun poured itself around me. The night before vaguely rendered into coherent dialect. I couldn't recall when it ended. I remembered the five-hour bus ride from Los Angeles to Vegas. The drinking. The good and bad dirty jokes. The singing. The dude with the dick nose on his face,

and how silly he looked. I remembered my shirt coming up from my pants. I kept pushing it in, but the shirt kept coming up. I remembered Sylvia, the one I loved because everybody did. I remembered how she kept issuing rum into my cup. How I wanted to lay my face on her neck and just leave it there. I recalled the casinos. The slot machines beckoning like whores. The old people dying in their bones. The serious players in cowboy hats. The steelworkers and the rankled businessmen. The blustery group of Blacks from East St. Louis. I also remembered Sylvia daring me to jump into a motel swimming pool, and for some reason I said no as if I had some sense. But somewhere between an image of a run in with some vato who in my mind had designs on Sylvia, and a walk I managed to make down the carpet-strewn sidewalks of the strip, with a woman in my arms—was it Sylvia?—to when nothing comes to me, I ended up on this lawn. Strangers kept vigil above me, but nobody came close or offered me a hand or asked what the hell I was doing there. I laid there a long time before I gathered the strength to get up, barely wipe the dirt off my pants, and follow the parade to the casino's killing floors.

There is a sense of having possessed
a deep something,
a beautiful something,
and having it stolen.
As a child I felt spent, useless.
But beneath all this, I had it.
Somewhere, sometime. Perhaps as an infant
suckling by my mother, or shining in the glow
of a rare smile from my father,
or just enjoying a piercing instant
of glee—but now it seems so far away.
I can't escape the thought; it lingers
around, itching behind my skull,
this inescapable awareness that I had it once
and it was taken away.

5. My Cherokee friend, Fourkiller, barely showed up for work at the Bethlehem Steel Mill. We were part of the "oil gang," a position officially

known as "oiler & greaser." Our weapons were grease guns, manual and air-powered, and various wrenches and pipe cutters. We greased the bearings, joints, shafts, couplings, and moving parts of all the machines in the plant. Considered the low men in the maintenance crews, we were also essential to every operation. "Hey grease monkey, we got a job for you," one of the millwrights yelled into the oil shanty where three of us were changing into our work gear. "We ain't grease monkeys," replied Bosch, another member of the "gang." "We're 'lubrication specialists.'" Fourkiller may not have been the hardest working crew member, but he was clearly the smartest. He seemed to master every intricate aspect of the fine art of greasin'. He had come from Oklahoma, joining with other Indians from throughout the Southwest as well as the few Mexicans and Blacks able to snatch some set-aside jobs due to a consent decree against the white-only traditions of the repair crews (some of the best paying jobs in the mill). Fourkiller knew his shit, but he was hardly there. After work, on those days he did show up ("Glad you could join us," Bosch would say), we would go to a local bar that catered to the mill hands, particularly on pay days. George's was one of the better known hangouts. Men swarmed around the pool tables, many of them from the surrounding factories and warehouses. I was lousy at pool, mostly because my eyesight was far from 20-20. But we had a scam going, Fourkiller and me. He was a bona fide pool shark (he'd be good at anything if he hung around long enough). So the plan was that I would start to play, with my bad form and missed shots, to entice the hustlers. Once we got a game going, usually for beers, Fourkiller would then rack up the balls and knock them all in. This only lasted a few games, but by then we were beer-dead, and nothing mattered, even when some of them dudes jumped us from behind, cracking heads, and we landed in front of George's door just as the mill's air whistles called us back to work.

when the wasted poems become dawn and are not gray-speckled haze,
when the upholding structures collapse from their perjuries,
when the money-system no longer determines worth
and purgatory is no longer your driveway
when the factory-spawn stops lactating 'burbs,

whose milk is dioxin, drying up earth's blood,
when all value is inside of you,
when the wasteland's raped-terrain bursts green,
when the creative heart is the only blossoming

6. Weather comes first; Chicago winding itself through tissue and bone. The gray-stone and terra-cotta facades on buildings then wake you to artifice in motion. Finally, the alleys, strewn with the remains of weekend parties and weekday headaches, come around to grab you from behind. For a few years, I roamed the city's cobblestone paths below El train tracks and slippery sidewalks to poetry open mikes, to poetry slams, poetry beer busts. . . everything was poetry. This was good. Poetry was good. For once, I could get drunk and not have to push aside the art. It came out in violent bursts. Better than fighting. Chicago embraced them with a flirtatious wink. My poems were some of the same angst-filled lyrical blasts that seemed to consume us then, us black-garbed and oh-so-serious folk. But with me there was a twist (everybody needs a twist, a performance poet once told me): I came from L.A., South Central and East L.A. to be precise. I had trekked forth from streets that now burned, that now rudely tossed the bed out the window, that made everyone fear the mortal one, that angered up the blood. People were interested, although I once believed they would throw me out on my West Coast ass. Yet to me, East L.A. and Chicago were similar. People spoke to you. Families mattered. Sidewalk talk and stoop listening mattered. Being real mattered. Love and hurt and late-night quarrels and dancing babies and large wedding parties—these mattered. The gangs didn't bother me. The craziness creasing out of webbed eyes didn't bother me. Even the gunfire didn't bother me (although I've dodged a few fat ones in my time). Chicago welcomed the madness in flight that dwelled within. It heard my cries, and looked up. In bars it's hard to get anyone's attention. But that's the point, isn't it? If a poem works there, it can work anywhere (although, to a drunk, almost any word order can be a poem). So I made the rounds—to places with names like Weeds, The Bop Shop, The Get-Me-High, the Guild Complex, the Green Mill Lounge, Batteries Not Included, the Border Line—there was even a performance space called

Kill The Poets, which actually got some people upset as if somebody really meant to do that (although there were probably a few who did). We got to know each other pretty well, we wicked wordsmiths: our intonations, our not-so-subtle subtleties, our internal breathing. We got to know the sexual impulses beneath every line. We started our own institutions—there was already a Letter eX, a poet's gossip sheet, but also a Pissed Off Poets group, a Neutral Turf Poetry Festival, and Poetry-Beneath-The-Stars; there were poetry ensembles, poetry dance groups, poetry video shows, music and poetry, fish fries and poetry, and poetry lakefront readings. There were presses—Abrazo Press, Juggernaut Press, Mary Kuntz Press, Doublestar Press and of course, Tia Chucha Press, which I named for my favorite aunt. Once I was accused of being part of a poetry mafia, which is silly because there's no real money in poetry. Still I felt at home here. Right away. In the late 60s, East L.A.—for decades, the most violent community in the country—bloomed in art: murals on housing projects and taquerías, poetry and teatros, garage bands and musical mestizaje. Art and violence are diametrically opposed. This saved my life. And in the late 80s and early 90s, in Chicago, poetry did about the same. Finally, when the alcohol had long overcome the words, I even found the strength to let the drinking die and the poetry live again. I believe Chicago had a lot to do with this, this hard-drinking, lip-busting, loud-yelling place that imagined us as laureates. And even if this proves untrue, there's something about the way Chicago smiles on you that makes you believe almost anything.

Words for clouds to fall away
a kind of stuffed solitude
damning the voices that slice at my eyes
every book closes in on me
a constellation of minds to wrestle
swallowed up by dead pages
Oh, so many ways to go,
so many places to visit,
and not be found.

7. Wading through the lush of memory, through speechless seconds,
seeing myself on the backhand of past lives, crumbling emotions
surround me, as this obsessive and irresponsible poetry man beckons
to write. To tell truths. Oh such a liar! I'm just a sleeveless
jacket in a closet of worn clothes; I'm the incision of scarring verbs
across the faces of all my loves. This Mexican who is a stranger in Mexico,
this pocho who hates milk with his coffee, juice with his vodka, who speaks
English with an East L.A. accent and Spanish with an East L.A. accent.
This Tarahumara's lost son, this graveled tongue, this ghost
beneath every ruin, rising like jaguar's breath in a tropical storm.
All sacrifices reside in me, all jagged chests, all virgin hosts,
all warrior princes, all Malinches and Cualtemocs, residing in my lungs, filled
with the wreckage of two massive oceans, all bloods commingling,
this Moor whose poetry stains the library walls, this armor-plated,
mail-wearing, sword-thrusting, Andalusian who flew landward
through Iberian coasts and those of Anahuac.
I am Cortez's thigh, I am the African beard, I am the long, course hair
of Chichimeca skulls. I am Xicano poet, a musician who can't play music,
as a musician is a poet who works in another language;
There is a mixology of brews within me; I've tasted them all, still fermenting
as grass-high anxieties. I am rebel's pen, rebel's son,
father of revolution in verse. I am capitalism's angry Christ,
techno Quetzacoatl, toppling the temples
of modern thievery, of surplus value in word-art—
exploited, anointed, and perhaps double-jointed.
There's a brown Goddess in my eye, a Guadalupana for the broken red
earth. The sacred is too sacred for walled cathedrals,
for incensed and baroque martyrs in vested garbs, for pulpit schemers
and sweat lodge fakers and garbled spiritualists on the best selling lists.
I am disciple and elder. I am rockero and hip hop bandit,
rapping Aztlanese in-between brick-lined texts.
What do I know? What blazing knowledge can I spear?
Who can burn with me and not get burned?
Violence used to be great solace; alcohol my faithful collaborator, scratching
dank words from stale corners. Now there are whole cities in my gardens.

Azteca drums pulsing from my temples. Saxophone riffs streaming
from the sky like a waterfall into the canyons of my body.
Walls carry my name, walls and their luminant fractures.
Walk with me to the Maya. Walk with me along headstones of past
loves, past plans, long-gone junctures. Walk with me through the forest
of collective remembering, shamed and honored by the trees.
I'm no immigrant; I belong because I belong. I'm no shaggy stranger.
I'm the holy villain, the outlawed saint.
The most Godless and therefore dearest to the mystery.
Where suicide is not solution. Where poems
no longer puncture the phantoms.
Where walking with me is to become brethren to rain
and night sweats and the betrayed.

this disjointed sneering
this lifting of cranial foam
this museum of oppressions
this waiting to be held, to be a musical note
this coursing through a rapture of voices
this clogged heart in the traffic of hearts

LUIS J. RODRÍGUEZ is a recipient of a Lila Wallace-Reader's Digest Writers' Award, a Lannan Fellowship in Poetry, a National Association of Poetry Therapy Public Service Award and fellowships from the Illinois Arts Council. He is featured in the CD compilation "In Their Own Voices: A Century of Recorded Poetry," issued in 1996 by Rhino Records, and in "Making Peace," a 1997 PBS-TV series produced by Moira Productions for Independent Television Service. He is founder/director of Tía Chucha Press, a Chicago-based poetry press. Born on the Mexican-U.S. border and raised in Los Angeles, Luis now lives in Chicago where he has been active in that city's internationally-recognized poetry scene.

CURBSTONE PRESS, INC.

is a non-profit publishing house dedicated to literature that reflects a commitment to social change, with an emphasis on contemporary writing from Latin America and Latino communities in the United States. Curbstone presents writers who give voice to the unheard in a language that goes beyond denunciation to celebrate, honor and teach. Curbstone builds bridges between its writers and the public – from inner-city to rural areas, colleges to community centers, children to adults. Curbstone seeks out the highest aesthetic expression of the dedication to human rights and intercultural understanding: poetry, testimonies, novels, stories, children's books.

This mission requires more than just producing books. It requires ensuring that as many people as possible know about these books and read them. To achieve this, a large portion of Curbstone's schedule is dedicated to arranging tours and programs for its authors, working with public school and university teachers to enrich curricula, reaching out to underserved audiences by donating books and conducting readings and community programs, and promoting discussion in the media. It is only through these combined efforts that literature can truly make a difference.

Curbstone Press, like all non-profit presses, depends on the support of individuals, foundations, and government agencies to bring you, the reader, works of literary merit and social significance which might not find a place in profit-driven publishing channels, and to bring the authors and their books into communities across the country. Our sincere thanks to the many individuals who support this endeavor and to the following organizations, foundations and government agencies: Josef and Anni Albers Foundation, Connecticut Commission on the Arts, Connecticut Arts Endowment Fund, Connecticut Humanities Council, Lawson Valentine Foundation, Lila Wallace-Reader's Digest Fund, Andrew W. Mellon Foundation, National Endowment for the Arts, the Open Society Institute, Puffin Foundation, and the Samuel Rubin Foundation.

Please support Curbstone's efforts to present the diverse voices and views that make our culture richer. Tax-deductible donations can be made by check or credit card to Curbstone Press, 321 Jackson Street, Willimantic, CT 06226, ph: (860) 423-5110, fax: (860) 423-9242.